A GIFT FOR

_____

FROM

_____

DATE

_____

IF GOD GAVE YOUR GRADUATION SPEECH

UNFORGETTABLE WORDS OF WISDOM FROM THE
ONE WHO KNOWS EVERYTHING ABOUT YOU

IMAGINED BY

JAY PAYLEITNER

...inspired by life

Ellie Claire® Gift & Paper Expressions
Franklin, TN 37067
Ellie Claire is a registered trademark of Worthy Media, Inc.
EllieClaire.com

If God Gave Your Graduation Speech
© 2013 by Jay Payleitner
Publilshed by Ellie Claire, an imprint of Worthy Publishing
Group, a division of Worthy Media, Inc.

ISBN 978-1-60936-754-1

Cover and interior design by Greg Jackson | ThinkpenDesign.com

Cover and interior photography ©2013 Shutterstock

Printed in China

3 4 5 6 7 8 9 RRD 21 20 19 18 17 16

Dedicated with love
to my bride, Rita, and our eight kids.

The five God gave us to raise:
Alec, Randall, Max, Isaac, and Rae Anne.

And the three God blessed us
with through marriage:
Rachel, Lindsay, and Megan.

WHEN A
GREAT ADVENTURE
IS OFFERED, YOU
DON'T REFUSE IT.

AMELIA EARHART

IMAGINE

Imagine the Creator of the Universe stepping up to a celestial podium before a multitude of eager faces at your graduation. He looks out, smiles warmly, and delivers step-by-step instructions meant to guide you through the maze of your days.

His words flow with refreshing honesty, stunning intimacy, winsome humor, and a keen understanding of human nature. His larger-than-life figure signals a thumbs-up with one hand and wields a bolt of lightning with the other.

Before concluding, He will equip you to make brilliant decisions, release you to exercise your gift of free will, and forgive you in advance for the inevitable times when you fall far short of His standards. Because He knows everything about you, He is the perfect commencement speaker—delivering a perfect recipe for a perfect life.

Do you picture God wearing a professor's robe and mortarboard? Sure, why not, if that helps you take His words seriously.

More importantly, does He care deeply about the gathering of fresh graduates ready to go out and make the world a better place? You bet He does.

You are what He cares about most.

To be sure, the commencement address recorded in these pages is inspired. Not because of the publisher or human author. These words are prophetic, canonical, and revelational only because they are restatements of truths found in Scripture. The footnotes that accompany each passage reference back to biblical text.

Considering the source, the principles are timeless. But for you, they come at the exact right time.

Read it for yourself. Invite the words to penetrate your mind and heart. Imagine the voice of James Earl Jones, Charlton Heston, or Morgan Freeman if you must. But in the end, realize that like the Bible itself (and any good commencement address), it's meant to be taken personally.

My

beloved children.[1]

[1] But we know that there is only one God, the Father, who created everything, and we live for him. And there is only one Lord, Jesus Christ, through whom God made everything and through whom we have been given life.

1 CORINTHIANS 8:6

You should

see the view I have.[2]

[2] The eyes of the Lord search the whole earth in order to
strengthen those whose hearts are fully committed to him.
2 CHRONICLES 16:9

As I stand before

you, I see more than

just a sea of confident, smiling graduates looking simultaneously unified and diverse in your caps and gowns. I see more than the audience of your family who loves you and has supported you these many years. My view is more than this campus and this community, and goes far beyond the horizon. My view extends from yesterday to tomorrow and the day after and the day after. Into eternity.[3]

[3] You saw me before I was born. Every day of my life was recorded in your book. Every moment was laid out before a single day had passed.
PSALM 139:16

No,

on second thought,

you shouldn't see this view because it would blow your mind.[4]

[4] "For my thoughts are not your thoughts, neither are your ways my ways," declares the Lord. "As the heavens are higher than the earth, so are my ways higher than your ways and my thoughts than your thoughts."

ISAIAH 55:8–9 NIV

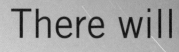

There will

come a day

when you will look back on your life and it will all make sense, but for now,

you'll just have to trust Me.[5]

[5] Now we see things imperfectly, like puzzling reflections in a mirror, but then we will see everything with perfect clarity. All that I know now is partial and incomplete, but then I will know everything completely, just as God now knows me completely.

1 CORINTHIANS 13:12

In this moment

see it all. Love. Marriage. Babies.

Lots of babies.

Even grandchildren and great-grandchildren.[6]

[6] Then God blessed them and said, "Be fruitful and multiply.
Fill the earth and govern it. Reign over the fish in the sea, the birds
in the sky, and all the animals that scurry along the ground."

GENESIS 1:28

I see friends old and new.

Sharing life.

I hear conversations that enrich and elevate. Many of you forming communities that create, worship, exhort, and encourage.

Together.[7]

[7] If we walk in the Light as He Himself is in the Light, we have fellowship with one another, and the blood of Jesus His Son cleanses us from all sin.
1 JOHN 1:7 NASB

In your future

I see adventure.

Goal setting. Risk taking.

Exploration. Missions. Enterprise. Passion.

Heroic achievement made possible only because of the courage to endure trials, failures, and naysayers.[8]

[8] Consider it pure joy, my brothers and sisters, whenever you face trials of many kinds, because you know that the testing of your faith produces perseverance. Let perseverance finish its work so that you may be mature and complete, not lacking anything.

JAMES 1:2-4 NIV

When you

follow in My footsteps,

I see innovation and revelation.
In art, music, technology, and science.

Words, images, and sounds. Tastes and styles.
Structures, inventions, and formulas.

Creations that never existed until you imagined them.
A gift from Me to you.

Some I will inspire in you in an instant. Most I will
inspire in you after years of study and exploration.[9]

[9] When I consider your heavens, the work of your fingers, the moon and the
stars, which you have set in place, what is mankind that you are mindful
of them, human beings that you care for them? You have made them a
little lower than the angels and crowned them with glory and honor.
PSALM 8:3-5 NIV

With great satisfaction,

I see moments of solitude and silence. Even as you graduate you've come to realize your education is far from over.

You continue to seek and find beauty,

truth,

and light.[10]

---

[10] Whatever is true, whatever is noble, whatever is right, whatever is pure, whatever is lovely, whatever is admirable—if anything is excellent or praiseworthy—think about such things.

PHILIPPIANS 4:8 NIV

As you awaken to

new discoveries and old truths,

you take the time necessary
to weigh the facts and discern

w i t h   w i s d o m . [11]

22

Don't hesitate to **talk to yourself.** [12]

[12] The heart of the righteous weighs its answers.
PROVERBS 15:28 NIV

More importantly,

don't hesitate to talk to Me. [13]

[13] Pray without ceasing.
I THESSALONIANS 5:17 NASB

As you find your place in

this world, I see you doing amazing things,

making your world a better place,

and—in humility and grace—

giving Me the credit![14]

[14] Let your light shine before men in such a way that they may see
your good works, and glorify your Father who is in heaven.

MATTHEW 5:16 NASB

27

You are feeding the hungry,
caring for orphans,
and making friends
with the forgotten and lonely.

You are giving new hope to those who have
made terrible mistakes and helping them to seek
and find forgiveness.[15]

[15] Learn to do good;
Seek justice,
Reprove the ruthless,
Defend the orphan,
Plead for the widow.
ISAIAH 1:17 NASB

I see you and you and you.

I know you so well.

I have called you.

You heard. You answered.[16]

[16] Do not be afraid, for I have ransomed you.
I have called you by name; you are mine.

ISAIAH 43:1

I see it all.

You are about to enter a new arena of life—
each carrying different potentials, but that's what
makes this scene so remarkable. Your individuality.

Your unique giftedness.[17]

[17] In his grace, God has given us different gifts for doing certain things well.
ROMANS 12:6

I could make a list of everything that needs doing.

And someone

here could do it.

SERVING.

GIVING.

TEACHING.

BUILDING.

LEADING.

ENCOURAGING.

BEFRIENDING.

Even seeing into the future.[18]

[18] If God has given you the ability to prophesy, speak
out with as much faith as God has given you. If your gift is serving
others, serve them well. If you are a teacher, teach well. If your gift is
to encourage others, be encouraging. If it is giving, give generously.
If God has given you leadership ability, take the responsibility seriously.
And if you have a gift for showing kindness to others, do it gladly.

ROMANS 12:6–8

Individually, you will go far.[19]

[19] For I can do everything through Christ, who gives me strength.
PHILIPPIANS 4:13

Collectively,
you cannot be stopped.[20]

[20] Make my joy complete by being of the same mind,
maintaining the same love, united in spirit, intent on one purpose.

PHILIPPIANS 2:2 NASB

To My great delight

am even joined in this view

by an impressive crowd of heroes from centuries past.
You can't see them, but they are cheering you on.[21]

[21] Therefore, since we are surrounded by such a huge crowd of
witnesses to the life of faith, let us strip off every weight that slows us
down, especially the sin that so easily trips us up. And let us run with
endurance the race God has set before us. We do this by keeping
our eyes on Jesus, the champion who initiates and perfects our faith.
Because of the joy awaiting him, he endured the cross, disregarding its
shame. Now he is seated in the place of honor beside God's throne.

HEBREWS 12:1–2

Their encouragement, along with your unswerving focus on the

...rize, will enable you to **run with confidence and perseverance.**

The rewards that await you are beyond imagination.[22]

[22] No eye has seen, no ear has heard, and no mind has imagined what God has prepared for those who love him.

1 CORINTHIANS 2:9

But, be warned. You are not home yet.

For now, you're still in a place of chaos, confusion, and temptation. In this fallen world, I am infinitely aware of tragedy, lives in disarray, and millions who don't know who I am. And it breaks My heart.[23]

Don't worry. I have an answer
for human suffering...

[23] [God] wants everyone to be saved and to understand the truth.
1 TIMOTHY 2:4

If you find yourself suffering because of wrong choices, bring your wrong choices to Me.

You will find forgiveness. [24]

[24] But if we confess our sins to him, he is faithful and just to forgive us our sins and to cleanse us from all wickedness.

1 JOHN 1:9

If you find yourself suffering because—in the

presence of evil—you have endured persecution for honoring My name, bring your persecution to Me.

You will find joy. [25]

[25] What blessings await you when people hate you and exclude you and mock you and curse you as evil because you follow the Son of Man. When that happens, be happy! Yes, leap for joy! For a great reward awaits you in heaven. And remember, their ancestors treated the ancient prophets that same way.

LUKE 6:22–23

If you find yourself suffering for no reason at all except that this world is far from perfect, bring your life to Me.

You will find peace. [26]

[26] [Jesus said,] "I have told you all this so that you may have peace in me. Here on earth you will have many trials and sorrows. But take heart, because I have overcome the world."

JOHN 16:33

If you see people in need of love and compassion,

bring My love to them.

Love conquers all.[27]

[27] Most important of all, continue to show deep love for each other, for love covers a multitude of sins.

1 PETER 4:8

When the time comes

o leave this earth,

I do see a place that is perfect. A place I have built for you. With lots and lots of room. It's My home and you're all welcome there. Consider this a standing invitation.

At just the right time, I'll be expecting you.[28]

[28] There is more than enough room in my Father's home. If this were not so, would I have told you that I am going to prepare a place for you? When everything is ready, I will come and get you, so that you will always be with me where I am.
JOHN 14:2–3

Trust Me

he days in your life and the life in your days will be exactly
right for each and every one of you. Your future is
carved on the palms of My hands.[29]

Like My friend Billy Graham said, "I've read the last
page of the Bible. It's all going to turn out all right."

Don't you love happy endings? I do.[30]

[29] I will not forget you! See, I have engraved you on the palms of my hands.
ISAIAH 49:15–16 NIV

[30] He will wipe away every tear from their eyes;
and there will no longer be any death.
REVELATION 21:4 NASB

But this is

not about endings.

This is your commencement. And as you commence into the world, you'll be glad to know that you don't have to go it alone. I will always be right here.[31]

---

[31] Be sure of this: I am with you always, even to the end of the age.
MATTHEW 28:20

And you'll

also be glad to know

that I have crafted an utterly thorough and alarmingly radical set of rules to guide you.[32]

[32] Your word is a lamp to guide my feet and a light for my path.
PSALM 119:105

But wait. Before you rebel over the very idea of rules...

Please remember who I am.

I love you. I know everything about you, and I still love you. I know everything you need, and only I can give it to you.[33]

[33] "For I know the plans I have for you," says the Lord. "They are plans for good and not for disaster, to give you a future and a hope."
JEREMIAH 29:11

So here are a few of those rules you'll want to apply

in the very near future. You don't have to take notes.

I've already written it all down for you...[34]

[34] All Scripture is inspired by God and is useful to teach us what is
true and to make us realize what is wrong in our lives. It corrects
us when we are wrong and teaches us to do what is right.
2 TIMOTHY 3:16

Because so many parents are in attendance

let's begin with a rule they'll appreciate:

Be excellent to your mom and dad.[35]

[35] Honor your father and mother. Then you will live a long,
full life in the land the Lord your God is giving you.

EXODUS 20:12

Here's another they'll like:

Don't waste your life. Or anyone else's.[36]

---

[36] Thou shalt not kill.

EXODUS 20:13 KJV

A few rules will make you easier to live with:

Whine less.[37]

Rage not.[38]

Listen more than you talk. Speak carefully.
Raise your voice rarely.[39]

[37] Do everything without grumbling or arguing.
PHILIPPIANS 2:14 NIV

[38] People with understanding control their anger;
a hot temper shows great foolishness.
PROVERBS 14:29

[39] The one who has knowledge uses words with restraint,
and whoever has understanding is even-tempered.
PROVERBS 17:27 NIV

A few rules will make you a better person:

Admit mistakes.[40]

Apologize often.[41]

Laugh.[42]

[40] Search me, O God, and know my heart; test me and know my anxious thoughts. Point out anything in me that offends you, and lead me along the path of everlasting life.
PSALM 139:23–24

[41] Confess your sins to one another, and pray for one another so that you may be healed. The effective prayer of a righteous man can accomplish much.
JAMES 5:16 NASB

[42] He will yet fill your mouth with laughter and your lips with shouts of joy.
JOB 8:21 NIV

And never forget that I am

eager to help you:

Bring Me your burdens.[43]

Bring Me your doubts.[44]

Bring Me your darkest fears.[45]

[43] Jesus said, "Come to me, all of you who are weary and carry heavy burdens, and I will give you rest."
MATTHEW 11:28

[44] Though the doors were locked, Jesus came and stood among them and said, "Peace be with you!" Then he said to Thomas, "Put your finger here; see my hands. Reach out your hand and put it into my side. Stop doubting and believe."
JOHN 20:26–27 NIV

[45] Even though I walk through the valley of the shadow of death, I fear no evil, for You are with me.
PSALM 23:4 NASB

When it comes to friends, coworkers, and acquaintances:

Don't go it alone.[46]

Hang out with people you trus

nd who will hold you accountable.[47]

Give credit to others.[48]

[46] If one person falls, the other can reach out and help.
But someone who falls alone is in real trouble.
ECCLESIASTES 4:10

[47] As iron sharpens iron, so one person sharpens another.
PROVERBS 27:17 NIV

[48] For all those who exalt themselves will be humbled,
and those who humble themselves will be exalted.
LUKE 14:11 NIV

Of course, there are a few rules

you've heard often but that really can't be emphasized enough:

Do the church thing.[49]

Break a sweat a couple times a week.[50]

Say no to that last slice of pizza and round of drinks.[51]

[49] Remember the Sabbath day by keeping it holy.
EXODUS 20:8 NIV

[50] I discipline my body like an athlete, training it to do what it should. Otherwise, I fear that after preaching to others I myself might be disqualified.
1 CORINTHIANS 9:27

[51] Do not join those who drink too much wine or gorge themselves on meat, for drunkards and gluttons become poor, and drowsiness clothes them in rags.
PROVERBS 23:20–21 NIV

This one you've also heard before:

Save sex for marriage.[52]

[52] Run from sexual sin! No other sin so clearly affects the body as this one does. For sexual immorality is a sin against your own body.... You do not belong to yourself, for God bought you with a high price. So you must honor God with your body.

1 CORINTHIANS 6:18–20

This one you may have never heard:

Sex is a gift from God and a gift to husbands and wives.[53]

---

[53] The husband should fulfill his wife's sexual needs, and the wife should fulfill her husband's needs. The wife gives authority over her body to her husband, and the husband gives authority over his body to his wife.

1 CORINTHIANS 7:3–4

There's a rumor that this generation is afraid

of hard work and expects to be given something for nothing.

Prove them wrong:

Don't be a slug.[54]

[54] A sluggard's appetite is never filled,
but the desires of the diligent are fully satisfied.
PROVERBS 13:4 NIV

When you get that first job,

don't act as if you run the place:

Make your boss's job easier,
not harder. That's the most effective
way to get ahead.[55]

[55] Have confidence in your leaders and submit to their authority, because
they keep watch over you as those who must give an account. Do this so that
their work will be a joy, not a burden, for that would be of no benefit to you.
HEBREWS 13:17 NIV

Starting with your very first paycheck:

Share.

And don't be surprised if it feels pretty good.[56]

[56] Give, and you will receive. Your gift will return to you in full—
pressed down, shaken together to make room for more,
running over, and poured into your lap. The amount you
give will determine the amount you get back.

LUKE 6:38

On the other hand, when cash flow is tight:

Don't be jealous of the fortunes of others.

That just drags you down.[57]

[57] For where you have envy and selfish ambition,
there you find disorder and every evil practice.

JAMES 3:16 NIV

And remember that ever

If it feels like you possess nothing, you still have the best thing:

All your "stuff" really has no long-term value.[58]

It's you that matters.

Your life, your hopes and dreams,

are what I care about.[59]

[58] For we brought nothing into the world, and we can take nothing out of it.

1 TIMOTHY 6:7 NIV

[59]Therefore, I urge you, brothers and sisters, in view of God's mercy, to offer your bodies as a living sacrifice, holy and pleasing to God—this is your true and proper worship.

ROMANS 12:1 NIV

What's more

when it feels as if you are less than nothing,

then you are finally ready for greatness.

It's a paradox. But if you surrender your broken life to Me, that's when your prolific life really begins.[60]

[60] Truly, truly, I say to you, unless a grain of wheat falls into the earth
and dies, it remains alone; but if it dies, it bears much fruit.

JOHN 12:24 NASB

Not just a rule,

this is a promise:

Your new life will yield a fresh harvest of love, joy, peace, patience, kindness, goodness, forgiveness, gentleness, and self-control.[61]

[61] The fruit of the Spirit is love, joy, peace, patience, kindness, goodness, faithfulness, gentleness, self-control.
GALATIANS 5:22–23 NASB

Bottom line:

Stay close to Me

and I'll protect you.[62]

And provide for you.[63]

Count on it.[64]

[62] Submit therefore to God. Resist the devil and he will flee from you.
JAMES 4:7 NASB

[63] God will generously provide all you need. Then you will always have everything you need and plenty left over to share with others.
2 CORINTHIANS 9:8

[64] He who trusts in the Lord will be exalted.
PROVERBS 29:25 NASB

Finally, graduates, I know well the questions
that resonate most profoundly in each of your hearts.

You stand at a

crossroads of your life.

You have choices to make.[65]

[65] Whether you turn to the right or to the left, your ears will hear a voice behind you, saying, "This is the way; walk in it."
ISAIAH 30:21 NIV

Your education—in the classroom, at home, and in life—

...as taught you to seek the right answers to the right questions:

"What is my calling?"

"Who/Where/When/How should I serve?"

"To what should I dedicate my life's work,
so that I can look back and see I made a
difference, living a life with no regrets?"[66]

[66] Therefore, my dear brothers and sisters, stand firm. Let nothing
move you. Always give yourselves fully to the work of the Lord,
because you know that your labor in the Lord is not in vain.
1 CORINTHIANS 15:58 NIV

What to do?

What to do?

Indeed, it's the right question to ask.[67]

[67] If you need wisdom, ask our generous God, and he will give it to you. He will not rebuke you for asking.

JAMES 1:5

The answer is **surprisingly simple.**[68]

[68] For God is not the author of confusion but of peace.
1 CORINTHIANS 14:33 NKJV

Of course, first

you need to be in sync with Me, My Son, and the Holy Spirit:

Put Me first. [69]

Live in My Word.[70]

Tune your **mind** and **heart** to the stirrings of the Holy Spirit within you.[71]

[71] When the Spirit of truth comes, he will guide you into all truth. He will not speak on his own but will tell you what he has heard. He will tell you about the future.

JOHN 16:13

Then…

And then...

Do whatever

your heart tells you to do. [72]

[72] Take delight in the Lord, and he will give you your heart's desires.
PSALM 37:4

Does that sound too easy?

Believe Me, **it's not.** Actually, **it's impossible.**
No human can get it right 100 percent of the time.[73]

But that's okay. I don't expect perfection.

[73] There is no one righteous, not even one.
ROMANS 3:10 NIV

All I really need is for you to see that

the answers you seek

cannot be found in this world.[74]

[74] Don't copy the behavior and customs of this world, but let God transform you into a new person by changing the way you think. Then you will learn to know God's will for you, which is good and pleasing and perfect.

ROMANS 12:2

In the end, remember simply this:

Tune your heart to the source of all power, grace, and truth.[75]

[75] May the grace of the Lord Jesus Christ, the love of God, and the fellowship of the Holy Spirit be with you all.

2 CORINTHIANS 13:14

☑ Put Me first.

☑ Live in Scripture.

☑ Listen to the Spirit.

Then follow your heart.[76]

[76] Trust in the Lord with all your heart and do not lean on your own understanding. In all your ways acknowledge Him, and He will make your paths straight.

PROVERBS 3:5-6 NASB

And you'll do great things.

I knew it the whole time.[77]

[77] For we are God's masterpiece. He has created us anew in Christ Jesus, so we can do the good things he planned for us long ago.

EPHESIANS 2:10

SCRIPTURE REFERENCES

Genesis 1:28 11

Exodus 20:8 79

Exodus 20:12 67

Exodus 20:13 69

2 Chronicles 16:9 03

Job 8:21 73

Psalm 8:3–5 17

Psalm 23:4 75

Psalm 37:4 117

Psalm 119:105 61

Psalm 119:130 111

Psalm 139:16 05

Psalm 139:23–24 73

Proverbs 3:5–6 125

Proverbs 13:4 85

Proverbs 14:29 71

Proverbs 15:28 23

Proverbs 17:27 71

Proverbs 23:20–21 79

Proverbs 27:17 77

Proverbs 29:25 99

Ecclesiastes 4:10 77

Isaiah 1:17 29

Isaiah 30:21 101

Isaiah 43:1 31

Isaiah 49:15–16 57

Isaiah 55:8–9 07

Jeremiah 29:11 63

Matthew 5:16 27

Matthew 6:33 109

Matthew 11:28 75

Matthew 28:20 59

Luke 6:22–23 49

Luke 6:38 89

Luke 14:11 77

John 1:14 111

John 12:24 95

John 14:2–3 55

John 16:13 113

John 16:33 51

John 20:26–27 75

Romans 3:10 119

Romans 12:1 93

Romans 12:2 121

Romans 12:6 33

Romans 12:6–8 35

1 Corinthians 2:9 43

1 Corinthians 6:18–20 81

1 Corinthians 7:3–4 83
1 Corinthians 8:6 01
1 Corinthians 9:27. 79
1 Corinthians 13:12. 09
1 Corinthians 14:33 107
1 Corinthians 15:58 103
2 Corinthians 9:8 99
2 Corinthians 13:14 123
Galatians 5:22–23. 97
Ephesians 2:10 127
Philippians 1:9–10 21
Philippians 2:2. 39
Philippians 2:14 71
Philippians 4:8 19
Philippians 4:13 37
1 Thessalonians 5:17. 25
1 Timothy 2:4 45
1 Timothy 6:7 93
2 Timothy 3:16 65
Hebrews 12:1–2 41
Hebrews 13:17 87
James 1:2–4 15
James 1:5 105
James 3:16. 91

James 4:7 99
James 5:16. 73
1 Peter 4:8 53
1 John 1:7 13
1 John 1:9 47
Revelation 21:4 57

ABOUT THE AUTHOR

JAY PAYLEITNER is a behind-the-scenes veteran of Christian radio serving as producer for *Josh McDowell Radio, Jesus Freaks Radio, Project Angel Tree* with Chuck Colson, and *Today's Father* for The National Center for Fathering. Jay is also the best-selling author of *52 Things Kids Need from a Dad, 52 Things Wives Need from Their Husbands,* and *One Minute Devotions for Dads,* and has been a guest on dozens of media outlets, including *Focus on the Family.* Jay and his high school sweetheart, Rita, make their home in the Chicago area where they've raised five great kids and loved on ten foster babies. You can read his weekly dadblog at jaypayleitner.com. Jay is also available to speak at men's event, parenting seminars...and graduations.

ALSO FROM JAY PAYLEITNER

Once Upon a Tandem

The One Year Life Verse Devotional

52 Things Kids Need from a Dad

365 Ways to Say "I Love You" to Your Kids

52 Things Wives Need from Their Husbands

One Minute Devotions for Dads

Do Something Beautiful

52 Things Daughters Need from Their Dad